LOST, DIVIDED & TOGETHER

GABRIEL CARRINGTON

Copyright © 2020
Gabriel Carrington
Lost, Divided & Together
All rights reserved.

No part of this publication may be reproduced, distributed, or transmitted in any form or by any means, including photocopying, recording, or other electronic or mechanical methods, without the prior written permission of the publisher, except in the case of brief quotations embodied in critical reviews and certain other non-commercial uses permitted by copyright law.

Gabriel Carrington

Printed in the United States of America
First Printing 2020
First Edition 2020

ISBN: 978-0-578-64706-7
Library of Congress Control Number: 2020904830

10 9 8 7 6 5 4 3 2 1

Requests for reprint or other non-educational use should be directed to Gabriel Carrington at gcarrington22@yahoo.com
Written requests can be mailed to Po Box 53326 Chicago,IL 60653.

Any resemblance to actual persons, living or dead, events, is entirely coincidental. The names and locales have been removed and/or changed to protect the anonymity of others.
Editor: Ann Downs
Cover Design: László Kiss
Front Cover Image: Abira Das

To all the single fathers, you are appreciated and loved.

A Collection Of 50 Poems

In Three Parts:

Lost, Divided & Together

Table of Contents

PART I: DIVIDED

    For the People 1

    Landlord 3

    Juice World 5

    Dear Ally 9

    Another Number 11

    Lemonade 13

    Long Bus Ride Home 15

    Sane 17

    Temporary People 19

    The Joneses 21

    Two Cousins 23

    Division 25

    Molly 27

    Time 29

    Difference 31

    You 33

    What's a Lady Supposed to Be 35

PART II: LOST

    Proud Black Woman 39

    Cancer 41

    The Life 43

    So Lost 45

    OD 47

    Mocha You 49

    Death 51

Drug Abuse 53
Darkness 55
Each Flesh 57
Empty 59
WW 61
Don't Judge Me 63
The Story of You and Me 65
You are Love 69
04-15-2018 71

PART III: TOGETHER

My People 75
Prayer 77
Auntie 79
It's Our Nation 81
Unexpected 85
Memories 87
My Body 89
Family of Letters 91
Unity 93
Dreams of Mother's and Father's 95
Wish 97
Technology 99
Stand 101
Greatest Lessons 103
Beautiful Black Boy 107
Ordinary 109
Connect 111

ABOUT THE AUTHOR 113
ACKNOWLEDGEMENT 115

PART I: DIVIDED

For the People

Social Politics -

Let's talk about this

Promising the People

What People?

Your People

Drug trafficking, unmarried sex, nuclear wars, racism

Is this your people?

Oh, we should stand for the people!

Help the people

What people?

The same people that spit in my face

People that tell me I'm not good enough

People that put this deep-rooted hate inside me

The people,

Her people,

Your people.

Fuck these people!

They ain't my people

Hating me, Hating you, Hating her,

Oh, so you light

Lighter than her

Lighter than him

Well, where's that ever got you?

Inflicted hate caused by the skin - I ain't!

Landlord

Rent is due on the first

My toilet been broke since the first

My sink is clogged, roaches up and down my walls,

Crack dealers dealing crack in all the halls

Sounds coming from in and out of my walls

Rent is due on the first

I make those calls

Every month, rent is paid on the first

Still making those calls

Landlord put me on hold on those calls

Rent is paid on the tenth

Landlord makes a call

"Rent is due on the first," landlord says in this call

Ring...ring...ring - I don't answer those calls

Knock...knock...knock - I won't answer at all

Juice World

I see you in my dreams,

Though I never met you.

Lingering near,

You are present.

You're still there; I feel your presence.

The lyrics to your songs play in my head.

What a sweet melody!

On repeat mode like a favorite song at a dance party.

On repeat mode like a love song.

On repeat mode like a breakup song to a heartbreak.

Why have you impacted me?

Why are you here visiting me?

I cried the other night,

Pitying myself.

Oh, pity me -

A loss that I didn't have.

I felt as if I knew you.

Directly, you touched me in ways that I have never been touched,

With words that seemed to assemble in my mind.

Your death devastated me.

It shocked me.

It propelled me to be an even better me.

Each breath taken away; it's hard to grasp reality.

The moment I turn on the channel,

Go on social media,

And see that you passed,

I felt like I knew you.

That never happened to me before.

Every word of your songs plays in my head.

I connected with you.

I vibed with you.

I leveled with you.

The other day, I woke up crying in a bit of sweat.

Your death connected me to the death of my cousin;

Your death connected me to what I thought is forever.

Forever is not promised to anyone, any man,

Any person, girl, boy, anybody - rich or famous.

Death doesn't discriminate.

Death comes as it is.

I won't discuss the circumstances of your death.

I'm overwhelmed from seeing social media dismantle your character.

Your choices may have not been the best, but then, whose choices are?

People throw stones.

People don't look in the mirror and see that they're the stones.

It's painful to listen to your music,

To hear the pain in your voice,

To hear the love in your voice,

To know that it all ended so soon.

My tears have faded, but you're still laying around in my brain.

You impacted me.

It hurt me to infinity, your passing, and though I never met you,

Just know that your music spoke to me in ways that I can't explain.

Just know that your spirit came to me in dreams.

Job well done - your art impacted another artist.

Job well done.

Rest in peace, Juice World, I will see in my dreams.

Dear Ally

I can feel your pain a million miles away.

No, I don't live in Hollywood and drive fast cars,

But I feel you yearn for him;

His touch,

Sweet whispers,

Rough cries,

Hard liquor.

The waves of the ocean transported you to me.

I feel every tear drop,

Every lonely emotion.

You are not alone.

He is always near.

Another Number

In unison we lay.

Your touch so gentle,

Caressing my bare breasts as your tongue intoxicates my mouth.

I feel every inch,

Every part of your manhood as my hand slides down your legs.

In between my thighs, you uncover my jews.

Giggling, I'm nervous as what's the next step to do - reassuring me that it's time...the wait is up.

You thrash me on my back as you make your way on top.

Unzipping your pants, you uncover your manhood; nervous chuckles, chuckles, I let out a moan.

Nervously, I blush - the day has finally come.

A maze of thoughts gather in my brain.

I'm nervous...a nervous wreck.

This is my first time.

You reassured me once more that you will be gentle.

You reassured me once more that you deserve my gold.

I lay still, closing my eyes as you enter your manhood in me.

I lay still and bite my bottom lip as you slide your manhood in.

And just like that, my youth is gone.

And just like that, my innocence is gone.

And just like that, I've become a number to a lover with a thousand lovers under his belt.

Lemonade

I turn my lemons into lemonade.

I said...I turn my lemons into lemonade!

And said..fuck all you bum-ass niggas that didn't respect me!

Fuck all you two-timing, pill-poppin, bird-brain niggas that second guessed me!

You were never in it for me.

Yeah, I'm angry...

Mad!

Shooting shots.

No looking back.

You better check next time you think you gonna disrespect me.

I demand my respect!

I'm like heated ammunition in the middle of the war.

Yeah, you better think the next time you think you gone disrespect me.

Long Bus Ride Home

Today I was discouraged.

Bus ride home too long.

Fussing and yelling at the kids.

Chicago winters just not my thing.

Work wasn't hard,

Just not where I belong.

Repeat, repeat.

Tuesday through Saturday.

Repeat, repeat.

My schedule never changes.

Sane

I write to keep sane.

I write to be sane.

It's because I'm not sane.

Temporary People

Peace has rested upon these tiresome eyes.

Our paths are differently aligned.

The opposite of you used to be me.

Now, the marathon I'm running is just for me.

Your visions should never reflect me.

We walk the same streets,

Revealing different masks.

We shall never cross paths.

The Joneses

desperate for acceptance but no longer able to get by.
diamond rings, gold chains, sparkling things.
now you do the math.
keeping up with the Joneses got you looking like a real fool.
no food, cold food, hot plate.
dinner couldn't be served tonight.
it's all good.
you're no fool; you're walking around with the new jew's.
my, my, what a surprise!
you go to school with no food.
my, my, what's not a surprise!
you in school with the latest shoes.
desperate for the latest fashion but no longer able to get by.
not a soul knows your stomach's empty.
only you know those pockets are flimsy.
Chanel purses, Birkin bags, not a single dollar for gas.
you're no fool, though you're walking around in the latest shoes.

Two Cousins

There were two cousins.

One had a baby,

One went away.

There were two cousins.

One finished school,

One started dancing nude.

There were two cousins.

Their family danced and shouted with delight for

the cousin who finished school.

Their family whispered in despite for the cousin

dancing nude.

Dancing nude produced food.

Dancing nude gave her a name.

She took the name and went away.

Cousin who finished school always stood still and

wished she could.

Division

my heart beats faster every second

I'm with you.

the moment you touch me, it sends chills down my body,

creating this earthquake effect.

your touch does something to me.

the thought of you not being here frightens me.

the thought of you leaving me for her kills me.

and so, you've created this wedge between us.

the division,

your jealousy,

my own insecurities,

creates this mishap of uncertainties.

Molly

Molly had a heart –

James tore it apart.

Molly had a dream –

James diverted it.

Molly had a kid –

James moved away.

Time

Play with words,

Play with sentences,

Play with life and get sentenced!

Difference

I love how you make me feel!

When I see your smile,

Chills run down my side.

Quiet rides home, my mind is wandering,

In every different direction.

In every different direction we turn,

Every sign we cross,

My mind can't stop but wonder,

Of every line you have crossed.

You

You cut me -
Like a thief in the night.
I shall not speak.
I bleed red.
The cut's deep.
You violated me.
You exploited every inch of my body.
You left me with a family.
I'm unable to breathe.
I'm panicking.
Life is about choices,
These are your choices.
Yes, it's true.
It was all you.
You disregarded our family.
Piece by piece, you broke me,
Embarrassed me,
Humiliated me.
You, you, you, you...
It was all you.

What's a Lady Supposed to Be

I'm supposed to be a lady - that's what "they" tell me,

Measuring up to society's standard of what it

presumes me to be.

Dress like a lady.

Talk like a lady.

Put away your tom-boy pants.

Your toy Glock 9s,

And anything that resembles a man.

Pick up some heels.

'Hoe paint.

Go on your way.

Dress like a lady.

Act like a lady.

Society always tells me.

Bake a cake, do the laundry, raise these babies,

is how society sees me.

History won't repeat itself.

New history.

A New path.

Society can't condemn me.

For I chose the better path for me and only me.

PART II: LOST

Proud Black Woman

I AM A PROUD BLACK WOMAN!

I wear my hair all over my head.

My skin glorious, my body damaged.

I lay flat in the sand as the sun comes to an end.

I walk to my own tunes,

side to side, my hips sway,

As I make my way.

You should see how they look at me.

A BLACK STRONG WOMAN!

No one can tell me.

No one can tell me that the sun doesn't rise for me.

I AM A STRONG BLACK WOMAN!

Who doesn't need he

He can't control me.

I AM A PROUD BLACK WOMAN!

I scream!

As I deposit my six-figure checks.

That's why he can't control me –

I march to my own tunes,

I dance to my own groove,

I wear my hair how I see fit.

AND DAMAGE MY BODY ALONG THE WAY!

At night, I go home and lay alone,

BUT AGAIN, I AM A STRONG BLACK WOMAN!

Who marches to my own tone.

Cancer

Invitation to love.

But I'm too busy fighting my demons...

The Life

I can't understand why you chose the life;
It is nothing but lights, camera, action.

I can't understand why you chose to die.
Wasn't it enough to see him shot right by your side?
I picture your future laden with finer things.
Luxurious ties, business meetings, and board games.
I envision your things,
In my various dreams.
Isn't it enough to be engulfed with four concrete things?
This is the life you chose for yourself.
No longer able to see the simple things.
No longer able to breathe the same air as me.

I can't understand why you chose the life.
The affliction became a thrill to you.

I hear you rap loudly with your handshakes and slang.

I guess this is what you prevail to be.

I guess your future was never with me.

I can't understand why you chose the life.

I guess it wasn't meant for me.

So Lost

So lost in the reality that it could be more than a reality,

And oh, did I think it was more than a reality!

So despairing to hear those words plunge my ears when you say you do not care.

Putting up this emotional wall that you knock down

When you come in and out of my walls.

Fixated on the love that you give; the love that you have, the love that you allow.

Consuming me - my heart, my body, my soul, my love.

Pierce my heart like thorns to the brain.

Could it be that we weren't meant to be?

The agony of it all!

Could it be you weren't meant for me?

OD

Depression doesn't discriminate.

It seeps through your body,

Like an open wound,

Surrounded by the plague.

I stabbed my skin.

My body is numb.

The pain rejoices me.

Lukewarm water burns my cuts, oozes out blood.

The spider from outside my window crawls up my inner thighs.

I won't let out a scream.

The pain feels extraordinary.

Decomposing thoughts filter my unorthodox brain as the spider explores me.

How dare you take what didn't belong to you?

How dare you take my purity?

It wasn't owed to you.

I wasn't a willing participant.

You stole a piece that I won't get back.

You were a friend,

A homie.

You took what mattered.

My lifeless body lying there as you lust over me.

The spider exploring my body is no pain to me.

You violated your homie; it's all the pain to me.

I can't believe.

I can't believe.

You were my homie.

A friend to me.

No one knows anybody.

Mocha You

When I look at you, all I see is the beauty in your mocha skin.

Your bushy hair,

Your eyes so naive

Full of youth,

But you live a dark life.

Your truths come out after the hours when you hop in and out of rides.

Your truths come out at dark when you fornicate with every Tom, Dick, and Harry that tell you you're beautiful.

They see your flesh - I see the inner you.

The beauty beyond the beauty; you're so beautiful to me.

Your worth is more than fornication, in and out of penetration.

A dozen times you were lied to, made a fool of, but still I see the inner you.

The beauty beyond the beauty is beyond you.

Death

The sky is dark.

The birds are onyx.

No wind blowing.

Just an empty belly,

On a full night.

Walk past my mirror,

Decide tonight is the night,

Walk out my door,

Decide to fight this fight.

Death is death.

The worst part...

You took your own life.

It still touches my core.

Pulling at my flesh,

For you are no more.

Picture-perfect life,

Half smiles,

Lies are a shame.

It's make believe through these broken lenses.

The Bible says, "Your life shall perish in Hell."

Though it's written in stone,

It won't change the vigorous love

How could you leave this pain on us?

Drug Abuse

Popping pills,

Sniffing Coke,

Smoking a blunt,

Keeps me afloat.

Eases my mind.

Limits time.

My high

Has to come down.

Molly

Lean

A bottle of lean.

Just need a sip sip

Ease my pain.

Yes, it's time -

Pop a pill.

I live in a zoo -

One pop,

Two pop,

I live in a zoo.

Darkness

It's like I'm trapped in the ocean with nowhere to escape.

The closer I think I'm getting to shore, the deeper my body goes to the bottom.

As my body sinks deeper in the ocean, my hands and arms begin to give in,

For they are weak.

As I sink, the light begins to fade and the darkness appears.

My lifeless body know longer able to see the light.

As I go under the water, my mind wanders and sees my life,

And how I should have fought harder,

And never gave up.

You see, I gave up on life when I became pregnant at 17.

You see, I gave up on life when I was no longer able to trust the ones around me.

As I slowly die, I realize I died many years ago.

I gave up on life the minute my failed attempts never prospered.

Should I rise again to fight? But my arms and legs are so weak.

Shall I lay to rest in the ocean where my body is at peace?

Laying in the ocean...sinking closer and closer to my death.

Each Flesh

I'm erasing the pain that you did to me.

I'm erasing the pain that you did to me.

with each flesh, I forget the rest

with each body, it does something to me

How could I be the same when you were the one that did it to me?

It's been in me all alone.

Screaming to come out.

I finally released the pain that you did to me.

We could have had it all, but you ruined the innocence in me.

Empty

never knew how someone could do such a

good job pretending

what's not said doesn't need to be.

I'm saying goodbye.

leaving you as you always leave me -

EMPTY!

WW

WW lays on my hand.

Imprinted in the melan in my skin.

Your initials engraved within me -

a badge of honor,

a trophy.

I wear it proudly.

You will always be a part of me.

Don't Judge Me

Used to be a different me

Now I don't care

if I pop pills

smoke crack

I just do me

Used to love boys

Now I kiss girls

and I don't care who sees me

Don't judge me -

you would do you, if you were me

Used to be so full of destiny

Now I chase men and drink hen

but again, please don't judge me

The Story of You and Me

I can't remember the first time he hit or the second.

All I can remember is the way the blade of his knuckle grazed my jaw.

Ringing bells sent alarms throughout my body.

Shock displaced my timid body.

I no longer myself.

Unable to move, I lay still.

Hot tears began to roam down my swollen face.

My eyes closed, closed tightly, the mind wanders to a different day.

A little girl emerges, full of smiles.

She tells everyone what she wants to be -

Running around in her mind, the little girl says what she will be,

"I want to be a writer," the little girl replies, so very full of smiles.

"Wake up," he shouted, in a caring tone.

"I'm sorry," he said, with tears peering down his reluctant face.

A demon of his environment,

He shed no light on love.

Broken jaw.

Bruised body.

Her mind in disarray.

Staggering apologies formed upon his lips.

Unable to control his anger.

His violent attempts to get her to understand the deep-rooted emotions from him to her.

How could he explain this?

How could she not understand his love?

She had to understand!

Tear after tear covered her bruised face as she kissed his lips.

She decided to stay.

A product of her environment.

What else did she know?

Broken relationships after broken,

Bruise after bruise.

"There would be no more hitting," he said.

"Never again will I hit you," he shouted with confidence.

"Until next time," she replied with open arms.

You are Love

I weep with my shallow eyes,

For I would never get to meet you.

I weep with my desperate cries,

For I never meant to hurt you.

You were formed with love.

Or maybe your father didn't want you.

Your mother's desperate attempts.

Your father's exhausted sighs.

You were made from the pit of my spine.

Two tormented souls forming this magical creation.

No ball games, first school dance, or wedding bells rang.

Your mom loved

Your daddy...

The two made you, but didn't know how to raise you.

The breath of life would never reach your tiny nostrils.

I weep knowing I have sinned.

I weep knowing I will never get to know you.

You were loved despite...

04-15-2018

For you were my heart.

For you, I would have done anything;

For you, I would have raced to the moon,

Jumped on top of the stars,

Just to give you everything.

It sounds so simple,

When really, it's complex.

For you, I would have done just about anything!

PART III: TOGETHER

My People

Coming from the palms of my hands,

I felt a different day.

Coming from the roots of my ancestors.

I fight for a new day.

New days with no oppression.

My people must stand for this new day.

Create a new way.

A way of utilizing the system,

To better bestow upon us,

Not conform us.

We must rise to the occasion -

We must become the F in freedom -

We must become M in Malcolm,

Who rambunctiously fought for us.

We must do away with the government assistance.

We must transform into business owners.

Not surprised by the luxurious brands - which brands should be no surprise.

We've been branded for years.

Brands of shoes,

Brands of clothes,

Brands of the slave master as he whipped his brand into us.

My people, we must fight for a different day.

A day where we own our own,

A day where we decide to remove this falsified hate.

Wake up, my people! Do you see the day?

Prayer

Oh, dear God -

I have sin.

Oh, dear God -

Please don't bury me,

Next to them,

For I have sin!

Father, forgive me,

Oh, Father, raise me to the top,

Where I wanna be.

Auntie

My deepest memories of you are the purist,

I can remember.

You watched me grow from a child - so sweet and innocent

To the woman I am today.

Holding my hand, you watched me down the street.

Walking me through the major steps of youth.

You took the time to plant the seed.

You watched it grow.

Now look at me!

I am everything you wanted me to be.

I am beautiful,

I am me,

I am intelligent.

I am that seed you watched grow 26 years ago.

Now look at me!

Are you proud, Auntie?

It's Our Nation

I'm proud to be an American.

I shout it from the rooftops.

I am an American citizen.

Proud to be a part of the greatest country that I know.

The government has divided us,

Split into two pieces.

I stand with my nation as the violence rises against our people.

We are all American citizens; proud we should be.

A country that is so great that a man who is a drug dealer

Can rise to fame and become a millionaire.

A country so great that a young woman who gets food stamps

Can become a best-selling author.

I stand with this country.

The government has silenced us.

Dividing you from me and me from you, simply because of the melan in my skin.

Racism does exist!

That's a path that we should align ourselves without;

Our forefather's sin.

Current white people don't apologize for what your forefathers did.

Current white people make a change within yourselves.

You can't change what your forefathers created;

You can change, among yourselves, what you create for the next generation.

The government has oppressed us.

The government has made us believe such defamed lies.

We the people run this nation - not the government.

We the people can make the change - not the government.

We the people don't need a government.

We the people need to wake up.

We the people need to see through it all,

The deceitful lies of our judicial system.

We the people need to learn the political agendas of the people we put in office.

Stand together, Nation.

Black, White, Asians, Hispanics.

If we stand together, we the people will never fall.

Unexpected

Take a break from life

Take a break from love

Take a break from me

Oh, who have I become?

Memories

The love still flourishes within me -

Like the birds to the trees,

The wind to the earth.

How could I forget thee?

Our love is still within me.

As time progresses,

The seasons change.

The moments we shared,

Remains.

Your face still haunts my dreams.

Your touch,

Still as our first time.

Your body lay next to mine.

I still feel you near.

Our memories will always be history to me.

My Body

My body is no toy.

My body is no playground for any kid to have their way.

My body is latitude,

My body is ownership,

My body is spoken for.

My body is not to be a shame for all the shameless men who've had their way.

My body is to be respected,

Not to be belittled.

I've finally found my way,

Now I'm here to say,

My body is mine,

and I shall be respected!

Family of Letters

A is for "effort" my daughter told me.

B is for "be better" my son hissed.

C is for "can't you try to do it again?" my husband tells me.

D for "damned if I do, damned if I don't" I think to myself.

They all judge me.

Unity

No, I don't love you.

I love the idea of what it's like to have a family.

mom and dad residing in the same unit.

papa going to work,

momma greeting him with a kiss.

I wish you loved me.

how I loved you!

then, maybe we could have been a family.

no, I don't love you.

just silly thoughts that it could have been me and you.

Dreams of Mother's and Father's

These dreams were not meant to perish.

dreams of a mother & father

making their way together.

these families shall not part.

a father belongs to a family

like a bullet belongs to a gun;

a mother belongs to her family

like a cub belongs to his hub.

a family was meant to be a mother and father in unity.

Wish

The silliness of your laugh,

The freckles on your face,

The stamina of your presence,

Speak volumes to your guest.

For oh, how I wish just one day with you!

You see, it caught me by surprise,

That storm that never survives.

Dark clouds.

Shadow skies.

Cold rain vibrated against my windows.

Weeping eyes - we've seen it all.

For oh, how I wish just one day with you!

Technology

Robots will take the place of us.

Everywhere you look.

We are phasing out;

They are phasing in.

We are to blame.

Our devices.

I ride on the train

Everyone is deeply engrossed

Their devices.

Their cool devices.

Speedy checkout lanes – high, fast Internet.

Deliveries.

Fast, Fast, Fast!

Fast as a pen drops to the ground.

We want now.

Instantaneously robots have already phased in.

Stand

You play games

You tell lies

But you could never

Tell I was "thee" prize

You had it all figured out -

Big shot

Boasting and bragging

About how your bag is bigger than mine

Your tiny thoughts

Your vicious lies

Will never stand

My awards hang within me.

Greatest Lessons

Greatest gift from God was the lessons he taught me.

I remember those nights not so long-ago thinking, "Is anyone there?"

Impacted so many people's lives yet they showed, not a trace, I was there.

I still cry out and shout,

"Is anyone there?"

Greatest gift from God was the lessons he taught me.

Not once did they show me a care.

Poverty is what I was raised in,

Financial literacy is what I came in.

Past due notices opened doors to new neighborhoods.

Conflicted by the bad choices,

Searching for love,

When they never cared.

Meeting the one who played me so cold.

Meeting the one again who hit me so hard.

Searching for acceptance in a world of unacceptance.

Seeking validation in people who never cared.

My love for them was just an opportunity.

I still shout out sometimes and cry, "Is anyone there?"

Manifesting love for individuals who never cared.

I cry from the pit of my soul for Wes and Charlie,

For a path of injustice they face in society.

I cry for their futures and mine.

I cry because they will be doing more than nine.

Suppressed by the time I wasted on people who altered my mind.

Not one of those individuals thanked me,

Not one of those individuals loved me.

It was God who opened my eyes to the greatest lessons in life.

The road was dark, turned light.

The path of loneliness struck,

The light flickered on.

With lights they all faded.

How dare they not see the glory in me!

How dare they not see the love!

It was God who opened my eyes to the greatest lesson of all...

And that greatest lesson was me.

Beautiful Black Boy

Beautiful black boy, don't you know who you are?

Beautiful black boy, don't you know how great you are?

You are the chosen one!

Never be afraid.

It is he who leads your way.

Beautiful black boy, who conquers all.

Your looks are visionary.

You shine light-years above time.

Ordinary

My mind is lost...

living in this ordinary world,

in this ordinary life,

with these ordinary girls,

working this ordinary job,

with these ordinary clothes,

driving an ordinary car.

Tired of living in this ordinary world...

Connect

Connections are made available to keep the internet on.

Connects to power,

Power into sockets,

Lights the entire living room.

How come when "they" talking about connections,

They don't mention the disconnect?

I'm involuntarily disconnecting the connection of what it's like to live this lie.

ABOUT THE AUTHOR

Gabriel Carrington, was born and raised in Chicago, Illinois, she is a poet, writer, and author. Gabriel, took a liking to writing early on and started writing at the age of eight. She is a mother of two beautiful children. When she's not writing she enjoys spending her time traveling the world.

ACKNOWLEDGEMENTS

In loving & memory of Johnny Neal, your spirit will always remain around me.

To my beautiful kids Luke and Leia, you are the stars to my moon.

Thanks to all those who supported, advised, and offered both praise and criticism during the creation of this work of art. This book was made from many different stages throughout my life. I thank you for your support and as always blessings to you.

www.ingramcontent.com/pod-product-compliance
Lightning Source LLC
Chambersburg PA
CBHW060200050426
42446CB00013B/2924